W9-DJO-414

Silence Spoken Here

Other Books by Samuel Hazo

POETRY
Discovery
The Quiet Wars
Listen with the Eye
My Sons in God
Blood Rights
Twelve Poems
Once for the Last Bandit
Quartered
To Paris
Thank a Bored Angel
The Color of Reluctance
Nightwords

TRANSLATIONS
The Blood of Adonis
The Growl of Deeper Waters
Transformations of the Lover

CRITICISM
Smithereened Apart: A Critique of Hart Crane

FICTION
Inscripts
The Very Fall of the Sun
The Wanton Summer Air

ESSAYS
The Feast of Icarus
The Pittsburgh That Starts Within You

Samuel Hazo

Silence Spoken Here

The Marlboro Press
Marlboro, Vermont

Acknowledgment is made to the following publications
in which some of these poems originally appeared:

The American Scholar
And Not Surrender
Cedar Rock
Commonweal
The Critic
Crosscurrents
The Greenfield Review
John Ciardi: A Measure of the Man
Sagetrieb
Tar River Poetry

Manufactured in the United States of America

Library of Congress Catalog Card Number 88-60731

Cloth: ISBN 0-910395-38-1
Paper: ISBN 0-910395-39-X

For Mary Anne, the rememberer,
and Sam, the happener

Contents

Silence Spoken Here

Silence Spoken Here

What absence only can create
    needs absence to create it.
Split by deaths or distances,
    we all survive like exiles
    from the time at hand, living
    where love leads us for love's
    reasons.
              We tell ourselves
    that life, if anywhere, is there.
Why isn't it?
              What keeps us
    hostages to elsewhere?
                  The dead
    possess us when they choose.
The far stay nearer than we know
    they are.
             We taste the way
    they talk, remember everything
    they've yet to tell us, dream
    them home and young again
    from countries they will never leave.
With friends it's worse and better.
Together, we regret the times
    we were apart.
             Apart, we're
    more together than we are
    together.
             We say that losing
    those we love to living
    is the price of loving.
                We say
    such honest lies because
    we must—because we have
    no choices.

Face to face
we say them, but our eyes
have different voices.

I *Ahead of Disappearances*

No Is the Father of Yes

I'm tired of living for tomorrow's
    headlines, tired of explanations,
    tired of letters that begin "Dear
    patriot . . ." or else "You may
    already be the winner of . . ."
I'm near the point where nothing's
    worth the time.
                    The causes
    I believe in rarely win.
The men and women I admire
    most are quietly ignored.
What's called "the infinite
    progression of the negative" assumes
    if I can count to minus seven,
    I can count to minus seven
    million, which means the bad
    can certainly be worse, and that
    the worse can certainly et cetera . . .
Regardless, I believe
    that something in me always was
    and will be what I am.
I make each day my revolution.
Each revolution is a wheel's full
    turn where nothing seems the same
    while everything's no different.
I want to shout in every dialect
    of silence that the world we dream
    is what the world becomes,
    and what the world's become
    is there for anyone's re-dreaming.
Even the vanishing of facts
    demands a consecration: the uncolor
    of champagne, the way that presidential
    signatures remind me of a heartbeat's

dying scrawl across a monitor,
the languages that earlobes speak
when centered by enunciating pearls,
the sculpture of a limply belted
dress, the instant of bite
when grapes taste grape.

                              The range
of plus is no less infinite
than minus . . .

                    I learn that going
on means coming back
and looking hard at just one thing.
That rosebush, for example.
A single rose on that bush.
The whiteness of that rose.

                              A petal
of that whiteness.

                         The tip
of that petal.

                         The curl of that tip.
And just like that the rose
in all its whiteness blooms
within me like a dream so true
that I can taste it.

                         And I do.

The Quiet Proofs of Love

"When your son has grown up, treat him like
your brother."
Arab Proverb

Don't wait for definitions.
                              I've had
     my fill of aftertalk
     and overtalk, of meanings that don't
     mean, of words not true
     enough to be invisible, of all
     those Januaries of the mind when
     everything that happens happens
     from the eyebrows up.
                              If truth
     is in the taste and not
     the telling, give me whatever
     is and cannot be again—
     like sherbet on the tongue, like love . . .
Paris defined is Paris
     lost, but Paris loved
     is always Orly in the rain,
     broiled pork and chestnuts
     near the Rue de Seine,
     the motorcade that sped de Gaulle
     himself through Montparnasse.
                              Viva
     the fool who said, "Show me
     a man who thinks, I'll show
     you a man who frowns."
                              Which
     reminds me of Andrew, learning
     to count by two's and asking,
     "Where is the end of counting?"
Let's settle for the salt and pepper

of the facts.
                    Oranges don't parse,
and no philosopher can translate
shoulders in defeat or how
it feels when luck's slim arrow
stops at you or why lovemaking's
not itself until it's made.
Let's breathe like fishermen who sit
    alone together on a dock
    and let the wind do all
    the talking.
                    That way we'll see
    that who we are is what
    we'll be hereafter.
                    We'll learn
    the bravery of trees that cannot
    know "the dice of God
    are always loaded."
                    We'll think
    of life as one long kiss
    since talk and kisses never mix.
We'll watch the architecture
    of the clouds create themselves
    like flames and disappear like laughter.

Wherever I Go Is Later

The sea's one season is the sea
    itself.
           Like sun or sky
    its only time is always
    yesterday forever.
               It rhymes with blood
    and all the blood's unreasons.
The lion's blood that lures me
    and the jealous blood of all
    my jackals waits in my own depths
    to drown me there.
               Each time
    I dive into those bluer, wider
    tides, I dive into myself.
The waves unbutton me and say
    that man's no more the measure
    now, that all is not reducible
    to reason.
           Leaving ashore
    the whistle's cop, the rifle's
    soldier and the building's lord,
    I kick my quick, spermatic way
    through words that wounded me . . .
"Please stay in Jordan . . . you will
    serve God better here."
               "Not
    her . . . not dead . . . O Sam, don't
    tell me that . . . my God, don't
    tell me that!"
           "We hiked up here
    last summer with a picnic lunch
    and played the best Greek music,
    and my mother danced."
             The words

re-live me as I float
two decades back or half
a hemisphere away.
                              She
of the thinking eyes, he
with just one poem to his name,
she with the freckled, serious
breasts and he who bled
as a marine . . .
                      The smoke of all
their voices blurs into the wind.
My wake pursues me like the man
I was and then dissolves
like snowing on the sea.
                              Swimming
inward to the loves I love,
the work that is my air
and a few dependable pleasures,
I stroke ahead of disappearances
that once were places I had
yet to see or faces
waiting to create me there.

Song for the Flies of Fire

The fifty-year-old girl of twenty
  said, "In love it's best
  to be cynical."
                 She'd modeled, acted
  in French commercials and sung
  Rock with a group called
  "Soviet Sex."
               Her eyes were cat's
  eyes but without the mystery.
Her smile faded like tired foam
  or like a memory of Berryman
  who, when all he spoke and wrote
  was poetry, decided he was through.
That's how it ends with some.
Burn fast, burn out. . .
                Even
  the repenters live cliches
  that guarantee oblivion.
                 Grundy,
  who put himself through college
  selling marijuana, prosecutes
  for Justice now in Washington.
Eldridge Cleaver shouts
  like Billy Sunday.
              Nixon's
  cronies milk the lecture
  circuit, publish fiction
  and believe with all their re-born
  might in President Jesus . . .
I think like this while watching
  lightning bugs play midnight
  tag around my house.
               Ignite
  and pause.

Ignite and pause—
each one its own Prometheus,
a sun in flight, a type
of Edison.
They burn like signals
hyphenated by the breath of night.
Each time I think they're burning out
instead of on, they burn again
like pulses that will just not die.
Their brightness lightens me.
It's no small thing to bear
a dawn within you.
It's
even more at midnight to create
with nothing but your being
and a light that tunes the darkness
something like the music of the sky.

Skyquake

A thunderbolt explodes like some
    enormous flashbulb
    or a detonating star.
                 It stalls
    the clocks the way shockwaves
    insult the dreams of reason
    to attention.
             The night spawns clean
    as dawn.
            Illuminated lawns
    shine greener than they are.
The not-yet murderers or saints
    are stopped in pre-murder
    or mid-grace until the night
    re-settles like an afterthought.
The lawns re-blacken, and the trees
    enshroud themselves like muffled
    flags at half-staff. . .
               I dream
    of other darknesses that stalled
    my fingerjoints around my pen.
I waited then for thunderbolts
    to loose the wordjam
    in my head into a mystery
    of sounds and silence on a page.
I wait for lightning now
    to fill the universe with all
    the light I need to see,
    to see. . .
            Beneath loud clouds
    a slashing exclamation point
    pretends the world starts now.
It strips it to its first
    and only form.

And then
the thunderburst.
And then the storm.

All the Medusas

Not that I'm lost.
                    I know
        the time of year, where north
        is, what it means to take
        the heat for some defeated cause
        and why I should give up cigars.
But these are trivia beside
        the possibilities.
                    Will there be
war?
            Will we be doomed
        like those foregone Chinese
        who lived to see their dreams
        come true?
                    Each time I'm told
        the peaceful must be strong
        and look ahead, I end
        by looking back and then around.
In country after country, hostages
        are human money.
                    Desperadoes
        who assassinate by bomb today
        and claim responsibility by phone
        tonight are no less desperate
        tomorrow.
                    As for myself,
        I fear the worst when governments
        square off with governments like rams
        about to butt, when generals
        play checkers on a map
        with someone else's sons,
        when honor means creating
        sorrow, funeral by funeral.
I know it takes more strategy

to write down what you feel
exactly as you feel it than
it takes to sink a ship.
I know that waste is both
the father and the son of violence.
But what I know and what
I should speak out in public
never match.
My students
arm me with their quiet soldiery.
Their eyes have more the bravery
of hope than all the rivalries
on earth. . .
To change my mood,
my son disarms me with a quote,
"Don't worry about everything;
nothing's going to be all right."
We laugh in rhyme before
the possibilities return like falcons,
and we frown.
They watch us
like watched clocks whose hands
stay always still.
They make us
stone as people being photographed
against their will.
They stare us down.

Unto the Islands

Each dawn I slew the sand
   behind Grand Case toward
   the cape where Jackie O
   is building her alternative.
                      Upbeach,
   two naked mermaids snorkle
   through the surf, their backs
   awash with oceansuds, their gleaming
   bottoms, like O'Murphy's, dolphining
   in tandem as their finned feet
   churn.
           A poem I've been planning
   pulls apart.
              The more I mine
   for nouns and fish for verbs
   the more it pulls apart.
                By noon
   the almost breathing sea assumes
   the fully female languor
   of a woman sleeping naked
   on a beach—her breasts re-shaping
   as she turns, her thighs dividing
   like abandonment itself, her mating
   slot so free of shame it shows
   its secret to the sun.
               I tell
   myself I'm here like Jackie O,
   and for a week it's true.
              The time
   is always sun o'clock, and every
   day is Sunday.
            The nights
   are stars and coffee and a netted
   bed.

19

But all around me live
black men with Dutch and French
and Spanish names and blood
so mixed that all the scars
of slavery bleed through.
                              Daily
they show me history in sepia.
That history's defunct and all
the slavers sunk, but still
the only church is Catholic Dutch.
The menus mimic Europe,
and a drunk whose middlename
is *van* distributes all the Heinekens
in town.
                              But who am I
to criticize?
                              An ex-colonial myself,
I can't distinguish custom
in my life from conscience, and I
end half-Calvinist half-hedonist
with nothing to confess but
contradiction.
                              Island or mainland,
what's the difference?
                              Until
a poem I cannot deny denudes
me into life, I'm just another
pilgrim passing through the obvious.
I need a true alternative
when now is never long
enough to write down what
I know.
                              Instead I stay a tan
away from who I was a hemisphere
ago.

I'm western history
revisited.

    I'm souvenirs and sun
revisited.

    I pay my way and go.

On the Stroke of Now

So what if I'm as old
        as Lincoln when he died, older
    than Shakespeare, twice older
    than the age of space, and three
    times Alexander's age when half
    the world was his?
                        My life's
    a place where clocks have neither
    hands nor faces, and the calendars
    are blank.
                    Besides, it's May.
The stars burn oldly new.
The seawarding rivers churn
    downcurrent with a muddier
    rush.
                    The mountains trigger
    fusillades whose green reminds me
    of a parrot's wing or of the sea-ring
    loosely noosing Curaçao.
Dizzy with daisies, the earth's
    aswirl in parables.
                        The purple
    resurrection of azaleas
    tells me that the pause between
    desires makes desire
    possible.
                    The blossoming quince
    confirms the everlasting once
    of wedding gowns and brides.
The buds that ripen into pears
    or tulips say what girls remember
    when the firm grapes of their breasts
    begin.
                    But why go on?

22

Beside this burgeoning the best
    of poetry is like the portrait
    of a room in which a mirror
    duplicates the room in which
    a smaller mirror duplicates
    a smaller room and so forth
    to infinity.
                    The smaller, the farther.
The farther, the more removed
    from everything that says
    what's best is better heard
    by saying less and seeing more. . .
I see too much to say.
                    This poem's
    in the flowers, not the words.

Clean Break

My ankle broke me when it broke
    and made me tell a different
    kind of time.
                  Baths were projects,
    stairs precipitous up or down,
    and crutches like the wings of penguins,
    second-rate but indispensable.
Asked, I told what happened
    with embellishments: the fall,
    the treatment in emergency, the splint,
    the X-rays, and the nurse's question
    just before the spinal and the surgery,
    "Which ankle are we fixing
    anyway?"
              A friend informed me
    that a skater cracked her leg
    my way, was splinted to the crotch
    and ended pregnant while recovering.
"Where there's a will, there's
    a way," she hummed.
                   "Where
    there's a way, there's a will,"
    I countered, pondering positions
    and the artistry in question.
                     Once
    home, I read *Ulysses*, grouted
    tiles and revered anew
    the names of Alexander Graham Bell
    and Thomas Edison and Clarence
    Fax, who housed our stereo
    accessibly.
              I re-evaluated friends
    and loved the good ones more,
    the better more so, and the best

ones most.
                    So many flowers
came I thought I died
until I realized death-flowers
molder with the dead while mine
bloomed on at home.
                    Harvey's card
was in-house made, but Mickey's
offered free the surest cure:
"Four parts gin, one part
vermouth, serve with olive,
repeat dosage until this recipe
becomes difficult to read."
Dr. Ward was not amused.
Having added three titanium
    screws to both my chemistry
    and weight, he counseled patience,
    caution and intelligent restraint.
I practiced these with moderate
    success until a telephoning
    priest reminded me, "Respect
    your doctor, or I'll kick your ass."
Thereafter, I obeyed.
                    Having
    watched collegians ride
    their crutches through the wind
    like skiers' poles, I vowed
    to stay advisedly incompetent.
That way if Mary Burnham
    cautioned me again to break
    a leg before I went on stage,
    I'd wink and say I did
    and wore a cast from Valentine's
    to Good Friday, conveniently
    parenthesizing love and death.
Then I'd tell her how

25

I rose in both my socks
in both my shoes and walked
like Jesus on the water back
to everything I did so easily
before that easy memory went crack.

The Cloak of Fortunatus

You left too soon so suddenly,
    and all your skill and wit
    and generous skulduggery went
    with you like a fire fading
    into smoke and back to air. . .
                               Just now
    your letter, written on your last
    live day, arrived.
                  It took
    the vengeance from your exit
    since you talked about "the next
    roller coaster ride" and thanked me
    for my thanks.
                "This, happily,
    seems to be my lot," you said
    with just the right degree
    of poise and peppery resilience.
Like any father, artist or perfectionist
    with more to do than time
    to do it, you did the best
    you could and left the rest
    to God and a martini.
                  "The cloak
    of Fortunatus," you resumed, "keeps
    one from being too annoyed
    and too frustrated."
                I checked
    the reference and came up dry
    and now prefer it unexplained.
But still it vexes me the way
    it vexes me to say that no one's
    life concludes as planned.
                  There's
    always something left undone,

unthought, untold, and we depart
unfinished as the world,
which goes on being what
we tried or failed to make it
while we had the chance.
Like Peter Sarkis, who could still
thank God the same for life
and dying, we can go in gratitude
for what we had.
                    Or we can fight
like Helen Middleton, who had
her hand still fisted, even
in the coffin.
                    Or we can leave
like you with all sails full.
But still we're missed as you are
missed right now.
                    I'm glad
we took the time to make
the most of time.
                    I'm proud
we worked where poetry and music
danced and kissed.
                    I'm grateful
for the said and unsaid words
and for the sung and unsung songs.
I only wish these lines
had never to be written, Ed.
No matter what they say,
they leave too much unsaid,
and still my hand's a fist.

                              For Edward Mattos

The Last Photograph of John Ciardi

It shows you at your best address—
   behind a podium and speaking
   poetry aloud, your own and Dante's.
Whoever heard you heard grandmothers
   praying in Italian, echoes
   of Pacific gunnery, the deft
   excoriation of the small of soul
   and how a word can grow
   through seven centuries, three
   languages and twenty dialects
   into itself.
             Prolific phonies
   bored you.
             Right-angled minds
   from Cambridge bored you more.
Chirpers from Manhattan and the Merritt
   Parkway bored you most.
                You
   left them to the pet awards
   they gave themselves and spoke
   an audience to birth that was
   too good for them. . .
             The language
   called American is less because
   you left it, John, but more
   because of what you left of it
   to us.
            I'm thinking of the poems,
   prose and conversations that were
   really conversations.
            Once
   we talked MacLeish—his boyhood
   voice, the perfect carpentry of how

he spoke, his utter lack of cant
or spite.
                   I told you that his
final words were to his son:
"You go along."
                     It made you think
of someone somewhere in the *Purgatorio*—
a warrior who died with half
the name of Mary on his lips. . .
But nowhere were you better
    than you were in repartee.
                         Offered
the *Obituary Journal* by a young
obituarian, you winked and said
it should give birth to *Son
of Obituary Journal.*
                    That brand
of Ciardi-ness will never die
as long as I'm alive to quote it. . .
After your death I heard your
    browser's voice on NPR.
"Good words to you," was how
    you closed.
                  Had you had time
ahead of time to choose last words,
you might have chosen those
to be your jauntiest goodbye.

Bare Beach

They're orphans here—each
    to his plot, all mothered
    by the same sun.
                    She
    of the blonde hair and black
    pubes keeps lotioning her
    appendectomy, her shaven thighs,
    the shifting jello of her breasts.
He of the Buddha-neck-and-gut
    blinks out to sea while spilling
    granules from a conch like grains
    from an hourglass.
              And so on
    down the sea-haired beach:
    four at naked poker, boys
    in a sandfight, redheads
    prone and oiled on their towels
    for "the total tan."
             The lax
    lions of their bodies proffer me
    the pro's and con's.
               Pro's:
    nothing hidden, nothing
    to hide—no chance of war
    since war depends on recognition
    of the enemy—love and shame
    are strangers in the world's bed.
Con's: at best a creed
    for the tropics—going native
    once is everybody's right
    to prove it can't be done—
    the first bee-bite on testicle
    or nipple, and the creed's kaput.
What draws them then?

                              Are they
          just hungering for how the body
          softens before sleep or after
          love?
                         Or are they simply
          tired of elevators, neckties,
          letters fluting down a wall-
          drop like shot birds
          plunging past a window?
If naked means "mistakenly
          unclothed," they're only half
          mistaken.
                         The other half
          is what I make of how
          they're made.
                         Among these clans
          who flaunt the common nationality
          of skin, I dawdle backward
          to Saroyan's law: "The egg's
          the perfect shape—the human
          head, the trunk, the breasts—
          all variations of the egg."
Studying some forked examples
          near the shore, I understand why
          men direct and women are
          these variations.
                         It follows
          from their architecture.
                                   In clothes
          they're differently alike
          as children of a single Eve.
All afternoon they loll and watch
          the tide repeat its only story
          like a stalled wall-calendar
          that says it's yesterday forever.

By sunfall, Eden's shadows
    track them to the clothes they've locked
    like laundry in their cars.
                                    To face
    the world's remembered nudities,
    they don its reasons, and they go.
Underwear and middlewear and outerwear.
Skin over skin over skin.

Lunch Is the Extension of Politics
by Other Means

"The guy who followed Bart's
        no speaker," quoth the Yalie,
        "twice I've heard him—like watching
        paint dry."
                        I think of what
        that means while watching Baby
        Doc Duvalier and his brood at table
        on the beach in Cannes—wife,
        sister, housemaid, bodyguard
        and children varying in tone
        from ebony to coffee.
                        BABY
        DOC WITH BABIES seems
        the perfect headline.
                        Younger
        than Farouk but more the patriarch,
        he faces days of grazing,
        tupping and lunching on champagne
        and ice cream with the resignation
        of a studhorse out to grass.
The tides repeat in unison
        the broken record of his life.
The anchored *Saratoga* helps
        recall his ransomers who let him
        keep the millions that will keep
        him king in Grasse or anywhere
        in perpetuity.
                        He knows they've
        pastured him like Marcos and the Shah.
He knows the whole scenario.
Act One's the love affair.
Act Two's the split.
                        Act Three?

34

Act Three is staring by the summer
at the tides—like watching paint dry.

At Sea on Land

Too far from shore to plot
    my course by land, too scarfed
    by fog to learn it from the stars,
    I feel adrift.
                  Wherever
    I was heading slides
    to pieces like the face of one
    long buried or no longer loved.
What matters most is knowing
    where I am and why
    and for how long.
                  Each day
    that's all I think about.
Until I tell myself I'm lost,
    I'm truly lost.
              Thereafter,
    I'm myself.
             I'm even more
    myself than ever since
    I now have time to be.
Old years return to me, old
    voices I condemn myself
    for not remembering, old
    places I could draw to scale
    from memory alone.
                    I'm
    like a man ambushed by love.
I can't contain my own
    discoveries.
            I live again
    just how it felt to smoke
    my pipe along the Rue de Seine,
    to speak my poems in Jerusalem
    and Athens and be understood,

to spend my Pittsburgh days
with Mary Anne and Sam and call
each day complete. . .
                        But back
to fact.
                I'm on my knees
right now uprooting clover,
shepherd's purse and chickweed
from the flowerbeds beside
our house.
                Soldier at sea
or sailor on seacoast,
what's the difference?
                        The earth
beneath my fingernails is still
my destination.
                        What am I
doing here uprooting gorse
and surge!
                Like art the work
is never perfect, never done
and never even partially
ignorable.
                I spot a single
cloverleaf I missed.
                        Live on,
rare weed.
                I spare thee.

37

The World That Lightning Makes

Under an upside-down
   and sooty ocean, I steer
   through summer thunder
   and the straight prose of rain.
A dashboard voice from Washington
   talks war in Lebanon. . .
                      Bursting
   like rocketry, a scar of fire
   slashes down the sky.
                   It noons
   the night and shocks me
   to a crawl.
              My car's a shelter
   under siege.
               The mean buttons
   of approaching headlights
   change into the always searching
   always aiming eyes of condors.
The lashing rainfall wails
   in Arabic for this Guernica
   in Beirut. . .
            I think of Lorca
   who believed the lightning-worlds
   of love and poetry could have
   no enemies.
            He never dreamed
   of lightning-chevrons on black
   shirts, lightning-wars
   and lightning-zigzags crayoned
   on a map that sparked a war that
   scarred a generation. . .
              This generation's
   condors thunder on another
   Spain.

The rain's a litany
of Lorcas bulldozed into pits.
The voice from Washington is no one's
and the world's.

Viva la muerte!

The Color of Reluctance

September, and the wild apple
   bowls its harvest down
   our drive.
            By ones the apples
   wobble to a rot-halt
   before I pitch them to the woods.
If "ripeness is all," I've had
   too much of all.
              The apples
   disagree and church me
   to their creed.
            "Why rush?
Winter will have us soon
   enough.
          We've weathered
   lightning and the blight.
              Slow

   deaths are all we ask."
Before they turn to sentinels,
   the trees in all their leafy
   languages agree.
           From green
   to cinnamon to blood to beige
   to brittle, they make the case
   for slowness.
           Slow as a wound. . .
Slow as the breath of sleepers. . .
They stand opposed to all
   that ended all at once in Sabra
   and Chatila and the south of France.
"Help us!
       They're killing
   everybody!"
         "I'm sad and empty,

40

Sam.
        You know how the princess
was nice."
                Unsuddenly as fall,
the apples bounce and dribble
to their rest like balls.
                        They speak
for dying young when you're
as old as possible, despite
the wind, despite the worst.
The last, high apple never falls.

Harpsong

Its green forepillar glistens
    clean as archery and surges
    forward like a keel.
                No harpist,
    I delivered it from junkdom
    for the plain geometry of how
    it curved.
              With scarce a string
    but Gaelic surely to its pins,
    my harp speaks more to me
    of Ireland than its flag.
                  I think
    of years when none could take
    by law from any Irish man
    his books, his sword, his harp.
I think of Cromwell's soldiers
    smashing first the harps
    in every Irish house
    to crush the spirit of "this rabble
    race."
            Poem or weapon,
    my *clarsach*'s both at once—
    something to pluck in peace,
    in war a prize that Cromwells
    break.
            It treasures in its every
    key the joy of sorrow
    and the grief of ecstasy.
               No wonder
    then I house it holy
    as a sword among my books
    for my and even Cromwell's sake.

Listening to What Was Here

The lamps wait to be helpful.
Geda's woodcut beckons me
    to look at it.
                The bed's
prepared for sleep or love or fever,
and the chairs around the table
stand like sentries at a vigil.
At home with all these presences,
    I see again that I'm
    alone with mystery, that I'm
    just learning what I've known
    forever, and that hell and history
    and heaven are, if anywhere,
    within me.
                That seen,
    I should be satisfied.
                    I'm not.
Tomorrow poisons me by proving
    nothing's what it is since
    everything is only what it will be.
The best prognostication is the one
    I've still to hear.
                The road
    I've never taken travels
    everywhere I've yet to go. . .
Since nothing but the future
    solves the future, I'm in check.
Yesterday's no help.
                And now's
    becoming yesterday as soon as
    it becomes today. . .
                Geda's
    "Homage to the Poet" comforts me
    in black and amber from its frame.

43

His poet's running with his house
in his head, his head in his hat,
and his hat on the top of his world.
Whatever's free is how he dreams.
And how he dreams is why
he runs.
And why he runs
is where the sun reserves
the prize of the horizon for the few
who know it never can be won.

Florence by Proxy

October's ochre changes
   everything to Italy.
                        Sunpainted
   walls remember villas
   near Fiesole.
                 I've never seen
   Fiesole.
            Some day I will,
   and it will seem a memory
   of noon in the United States
   when I became a Florentine
   because the sun bewildered me.
Who among the Florentines
   is listening?
               Who else but me
   who sees in the Italians
   the human race that Goethe
   saw. . .
            Today their cops
   are commodores; their Fiats,
   weapons in their whizzing duels
   on the road; their shoes and gloves,
   the very renaissance of calf.
Tribal to the death, they swear
   by their mothers, breastfeed
   their sons wherever, prefer
   their pasta three-fourths cooked,
   and sing whatever whenever. . .
Mistaken for Italian half
   my life, I'm of the tribe.
If it's Italian to speak
   in tears before goodbyes,
   I qualify.
             If it's Italian

to choose tomatoes one
by one, I qualify.
                              If it's
Italian to laugh when no one
else is laughing or to whistle
at the wheel, I qualify.
                              One
murmur in Italian soothes
the Florentine in me that French
confuses, German contradicts,
and Spanish misses by a hair.
One murmur, and I feel
   what Goethe felt when Florence
   wounded him with Italy
   for life though Goethe spent
   not quite three hours there.

A Deer among the Peppers

Nearing, the deer becomes
    a doe.
             She hoofs my yard
    before my interloper's eyes.
                        Swan-ing
    her neck, she nimbles woodward
    like a nude girl toeing
    a cold shore.
             The woods
    envelop her the way the sea
    awaits a swimmer.
                Slowly
    and swan-erect she goes.
                  The aura
    of herself goes with her.
Property lines assume
    their old priorities.
               The peppers
    lose at once their wildness,
    and the yard becomes another
    lawn that flows unbordered
    into other lawns like water
    into water into water.
                   No
    matter where I look
    or when, the lack is deer.

Diming

The twirled dime whirls
　　on its edge before it slurs
　　and slithers down to dime
　　again.
　　　　　Re-spun, it turns
　　from globe to planisphere
　　to wings awobble and awry
　　that hunger still for heaven.
Dime-drop or deathfall, which
　　am I watching?
　　　　　　　Turntabled
　　down to wonder, I absorb tomorrows
　　like a redwood, ring by ring.
Even when I'm still, I'm
　　turning.
　　　　　Turned, I'm still
　　en route to where I am.
　　　　　　　　Don't
　　ask me to explain.
　　　　　　　This dime
　　that is my toy explains. . .
It turns me like a poem
　　totally around until
　　it's always now or never.
Circle by circle, I re-create
　　creation in no image
　　but my own.
　　　　　A flag
　　that rolls like drowning laundry
　　in the rain, refusing not
　　to fly, becomes my flag.
A hooked fish twitching
　　in the choking sunlight fights
　　the fight I fight with all

48

that smothers me.
                        Don't ask
me to explain.
                        This dime
that is my toy explains.
Not yet the ground's, it spins
as long and far from zero
as it can.
                What makes
the poem makes the man.

King Nothing

"Black dog" was Churchill's
   phrase for what I'm facing
   here.
        I keep reporting
   to my desk, my pen, my books,
   but nothing comes of it.
I'm spared confirming Montesquieu's
   "A man can play the fool
   in everything but poetry."
I'm out of poetry right now.
Seamus would shrug and say,
   "When you have nothing to write,
   write nothing."
        Better than
   writing badly.
        Better than fraud.
On T-shirts, matchbooks and bumper
   stickers, fraud has risen
   to final solutions.
        "Send
   a Cuban home for Christmas!"
"Sickle cell anemia's
   the great white hope!"
"Arabs can go and reproduce
   themselves!"
        The isms
   in the words explode like spittle
   in my face. . .
        If all we do
   begins in our imagining, I should
   expect the worst more often than
   the best.
        It sells.
           It meets the needs

of hate.
It happens on command.
It lacks the lightning of the best,
which comes when it comes to write
the man the way a dance
will dance the dancers when the dance
is right.
Like love it lets
the eyes become the face's
sky again and takes us where
it takes us—never soon
enough but not too late.
As long as that's worth
waiting for, I'll wait.

Kak

Her heroines were Pola Negri,
    Gloria Swanson and Mae West—
    one for glamour, one for style,
    one for nerve.
                First on her scale
    of praise came courage of the heart,
    then brains, then something called
    in Arabic "lightbloodedness."
                       All
    birds but owls she loved, all
    that was green and growable,
    including weeds, all operas
    in Italian, the schmaltzier the better. . .
Lightning she feared, then age
    since people thought the old
    "unnecessary," then living on
    without us, then absolutely nothing.
Each time I'd say some girl
    had perfect legs, she'd tell me
    with a smile, "Marry
    her legs."
              Or if I'd find
    a project difficult, she'd say,
    "Your mother Lottie mastered
    Greek in seven months."
Or once when Maris bested Ruth's
    home runs by one, she said,
    "Compared to Ruth, who's Harris?"
Crying while she stitched my shirt,
    she said, "You don't know
    what to suffer is until
    someone you love is suffering
    to death, and what can you do?"
On principle she told one bishop

what she thought of him.
On personality she called one
    global thinker temporarily
    insane.
                She dealt a serious
    hand of poker, voted
    her last vote for Kennedy
    and wished me a son two years
    before he came.
                She hoped
    that she would never die
    in bed.
                And never she did.
"When you and your brother were young,"
    she said, "and I was working,
    then was I happy."
                And she was.
The folderol of funerals disgusted
    her enough to say, "I'm
    telling no one when
    I die."
                And she didn't.
One night she jotted down
    in longhand on a filing card,
    "I pray to God that I'll be
    with you always."
                And she is.

Anne's on Any Anniversary

Remember Canada?
                              We pooled
        our dollars and we went,
        relying only on each other
        and a car that had its problems.
Since then our counterpoints
        persist.
                        I hate fast
        and love slow while you're
        the opposite.
                              I'm Centigrade.
You're Fahrenheit.
                        I throw away.
You treasure.
                        I hear the words
        and trace the silhouettes.
                                  You learn
        the rhythm and enjoy the colors.
If every day's the picnic
        after Adam's dream, we're picnickers.
En route to anywhere, we bicker
        as we go but come home
        happy.
                        What bonds us then?
A love of figure-skating,
        manners, courage and the poetry
        of being kind?
                              Or just
        that difference makes no
        difference to the heart.
                                  Confirmed
        by how we faced three deaths
        together and a birth that answered
        everything, we're sure of nothing

but the going on.
                         We take
our chances like Freud's "group
of two" whose only books are stars
and waves and what the wind
is doing. . . .
                    Queen of the right
word and when it should be
said, I love you for the way
you keep surprising me by being
you.
              Who else could whisper
through the pentathol before
your surgery, "If anything goes
wrong, take care of Sam."
Then, to prove the woman in you
never sleeps, you added, "How
do I look?"
                   Darling, no wonder
every child and flower opens up
to you.
               You can't be unreceiving
or deceiving if you want to,
and you've yet to want to.
That's your mystery.
                          If "love
plus desperation equals poetry,"
then love plus mystery is all
the desperation I deserve to learn.
On cold nights or warm
   I'll turn and tell you this,
   not loud enough to wake you,
   but in secret, softly, like a kiss.

The First Thirtieth

If loving is "the laughter of two
    bodies," we've laughed a lot
    and loved it.
                But every laugh's
    the first for us as every
    breath or day or anniversary's
    the first.
             Who was it said
    that God despises those
    who count?
               Why bother over
    sums if marriage seems
    as briefly long as one full
    day and one short night?
Let all the counters count
    their way to June eleventh
    thirty years ago.
              They'll end
    with history, mere history,
    since all that counting does
    is lock you in the world.
For lovers, one plus one plus
    one add up to times
    when time's irrelevant since love
    has made them one another's time,
    and that's the time that keeps.
They feel the sleep of memory
    become today as quietly
    as all their words and whispers
    turn into the air.
              Flowers
    speak that language.
              And the wind.
And kisses when it makes

no difference where or why. . .
Over the Atlantic once
    I bought an in-flight watch
    that told and tells time twice—
    this minute and the time it is
    in Paris.
                    Let's call the time
    it is right now in Paris
    something like the time we tell.
Always differently identical,
    it happens orangely in Italy,
    olively in Egypt, orchidly
    in Monaco, crimsonly in Barcelona,
    silverly in London, greenly
    in Kilkenny, balsamly near Saranac
    and steady as the sun at home.
Even if it ends, we'll laugh
    and say we're still not done
    because we're only just beginning
    what we always have begun.

II *The Price of All Salvation*

Throes

To learn a woman, to memorize
    the glide of her breasts between
    her blouse's wings, to watch
    her deep in mother-thinking
    just before she sleeps. . .
                        These
are secrecies.
                She hides from you
the fear you've seen in fisherwives
who wait ashore alone
for men who farm or hunt
the sea.
           Tears are her truest
language, and all the dialects
of silence happen in her eyes.
Why should she tatter what
    she feels with talk?
                Facing
her body's face, you see
her be the woman she might be
when showering or swirling
in a waltz of dreams or waking
naked to the naked sun
in Tuscany.
            If you say only
what evades you in the saying,
she will hear you to the end.
Because she knows that love
    means joining loneliness
    to loneliness to make one
    solitude, she seems like one
    remembering the future

and distrusting it.
How can she
tell you this?
Or why?
Or when?

2

Dancing, you forget how
oakflakes fall and flatten
like a thousand duckprints
on October's lawn.
You forget
the poems you will never
write and everything that came
to you in dreams and left
in dreams.
You forget the dead
you'll both become and all
the dead your loving keeps
alive.
Like coupled nouns
you turn into the dancing verb
that's born and dies each time
you dance it.
Waist to waist,
you dance your world between
you and complete together all
you lack alone as steady
frictions make a single fire.
Don't think about the music.
You're the music!
Obey
your feet and dance until
your dancing proves that dance
and dancer are the same as love

and lovers when they meet.

3

In this new land your enemies
    are maps and almanacs
    and anything that counts the time.
Wounded with absence, you
    convalesce apart.
                    Each
    memory you made is like
    the Renaissance or the great age
of sail—unique but unrepeatable.
Alone, you're at the mercy
    of your eyes.
                    They never had
enough.
                    They spoke the only
    language you could understand.
Now blind and mute, you learn
    that loneliness and being left
    alone are unalike as twin
    from twin—not much, but enough.
If you explain your frowns
    to anyone but her, you might
    as well be speaking Japanese.
Some days are long held breaths. . .
Is this an exile or the way
    you'll be forever?
                    Why can't you
    be like gods who change
    into the wind and back
    to prove no loss is mortal
    but the last?
                    Where can you
    go if you possess within

yourselves each other's
compass and address?
                    Each thought's
a plan.
            Each plan's a loss. . .
You live as best you can.

4

You meet, and there's the sun
    again like God's first light.
Your blind eyes speak.
                    Your
    mute eyes read your
    facing faces.
                Sooner
    than the sudden rose of your
    first kiss, you solve each
    other with a look as perfectly
    as keys solve locks.
                        You toast
    from the same cup a time
    you're always just remembering
    as never time enough.

5

If you draw back from her,
    you see her nearer, clearer,
    dearer.
            Not what the Nikon
    sees—the wink when she wins,
    the caught curve of her smile,
    the way the least injustice
    cocks the trigger in her jaw.
Instead, you seem to see

64

the ache of no one there—
her dresses on their hangers
never to be worn again—
her mirror silent as an empty
stage—her side of the bed
like winter forever.
                    If that's
the risk, what's left but loving
as the last defiance?
                         Ongoing
as your blood, you live
uncornered in your cornered rooms
like paintings space alone
can frame.
              You let no more
than who you are come near you.
You say no less than what
you see, and nothing but
your eyes can hear you.

In a Frictionless Atmosphere
Whatever Moves Can Move Forever

Welcome to weightlessness where all
    the lights stay green, where space
    is squared, cubed and double-cubed,
    where you can sail like satellites
    or like the satellites inside of satellites
    as far as satellites can sail.
Just think of it!
                        Freewheeling
    for the frictionless!
                        While half
    the world survives on the addictive
    or superfluous, you'll learn the self-
    sufficiency of stars.
                        While agers
    grow in time to spend more time
    remembering than planning,
    you'll float as quietly and friction-
    free as soap on a slow slide.
Of course, what's sacrificed in this
    redemption is the life you thought
    was life before you opted out.
The friction of long thought
    will never show you how all
    diamonds start as coal.
                        The time
    of sweat will vanish like a dream.
Gone will be those midnights
    in the sack when frictioneers can frict.
And gone will be whatever rubs you
    wrong since where you'll always
    never be is nowhere, and there
    your life will stay ahead
    of you forever. . .

So what if Patrick
Henry spoke of liberty or death.
Perhaps he spoke for no one
but himself.
So what if Nadia
wrote her final book while cancer
silenced all she could have said
except, "I come to you
with tenderness."
She only proved
a million lifetimes aren't enough
to love even a small country.
So what if twenty-year-old
Espartaco stands right now
with his back to the chute where the bull
comes out.
Flourishing the red
song of his cape is just another
of his matadoring tricks to make
himself and all his fans believe
that living on's not everything.

After Which No Further Argument Is Possible

Best to admit it.
                              Poetry's
over.
              You hear yourself
repeating what you wrote
ten years ago—and not
as well.
                    Even with students
you discover ashes in your words.
"What's wrong with that?
                              We all
repeat ourselves."
                          You want
to say *that's* wrong with that.
The verses of Ecclesiastes warned
you to accept a time
for now, a time for then.
The problem is you can't
capitulate.
                    You sense how
certain women over fifty
feel—wanting children
they will never have.
                              It's
of a piece.
                    But something in you
says a harvest's in your future
if you're patient.
                          So you wait.
And wait.
              Perhaps you'll end
like Ezra in his dotage, mute
but always listening.
                              Or write

a book with nothing but
the alphabet on every page.
Asked why, you'll say that all
the poems anyone can dream
are there for the deciphering
while all the rest and best
stay lost like white on white
between the letters and the lines. . .
As for fatigue, there's no
escape.
                    You'll always be
composing in your head.
                              Don't
dream that traveling's a respite.
Or beliefs.
                    Or women veeing
out their legs for loving.
                              Nothing
will absolve you from short
days for long work.
                         Forget
the fops and all their valentines.
They only prove the well-dressed
corpse is for the dead to read.
Forget the tricks except those few
that stay invisible as nails
in furniture or stitches in a suit.
Assume that what you write
is not the way you learned
the world but how it's born
within you.
                    Re-name Australia.
Imitate Picasso sculpting
toros and their horns
from biker's seats and handlebars.
Imagine Venus with both arms

restored, her fingers shaping
dough into a loaf, her breasts
in sweat beneath an apron.
Describe how certain men
try on a woman with their eyes
for size or tell how dogs
run upstairs old and downstairs
young.
            If words are the black
keys, and pauses the white,
see poetry in every pause
as architects see architecture
in the space invented by a surface,
not the surface.
            As for yourself,
be arctic in July and tropical
at zero to be sure
your inspiration's more than
weather.
            Then be still
and listen while your pen's
small voice becomes a whisper
that becomes a mission
that becomes a master
that becomes a tyrant
that becomes the poem you've
been writing for the rest of your life.

Update

Trying to toughen where the hurt
   came once and where it stays,
   you learn too late that nothing
   heals, that years are poultices,
   not cauteries.
              It takes so little
for the scars to peel and show
the rawness, like a heart exposed
by surgery, alive and breathing
underneath.
          You say
you should have faced your fate
like Bernhardt in her pall and let
it purge you to the bones.
                But who cares
what you say?
          Like any general
preparing for a war that's past,
you train yourself for battles
you've already lost and call it
wisdom.
         Why can't you stop
and say instead the steady
present tense of suffering
is just too much for you?
Bernhardt in her nightly coffin
learned no more of readiness
from such rehearsals than the saints.
The death that Shakespeare said
you owe to God, you'll pay,
as she did, only once.
              But other
deaths comes first.
           The deaths

you eat to live are bearable:
the fresh deaths of greens,
the frozen deaths of hens,
the deathtaste in the serious cracker
that is Christ, the small deaths
you call goodbyes, the sweet
deaths that lovers die each time
they mate.
           The deaths that silence
you are those you thought
could never happen, but they did.
They leave you asking what
became of God.
               Midnights
are voids where sleep no longer
executes you into dawn but lets
you linger and survive.
                  By dark
you sweat the sweat of stones.
By light you doodle circles
on a pad to show yourself
that something still can be complete.
If you believe the "truest life"
is when you are in "dreams awake,"
your life is true beyond belief.
Your past is not your shadow
but yourself, and now will stay
right now until you die.

The Future's Still Behind You

Still conscious, still yourself, you know
    that something's changing you.
It speaks in dialects you've heard
    before and almost understand.
It spoke up first the day the chain
    peeled off the sprocket of your Schwinn
    and left you pumping backward
    forward while the bike veered on.
It spoke again the morning after
    the assassination when you awoke
    to find the future murdered
    with the President. . .
                    Because you trust
    more in belief than fact,
    you can't believe the fact
    that's overtaken you.
                Your body
understands.
              Like a good dog
it tends to itself.
            It starts
to heal while you're too busy
not accepting what you must
accept.
          Tonight you know
the mood of soldiers stationed
hemispheres from home on Christmas
Eve.
      You're lost like someone
mapless in the endlessness
of Texas on a night without stars.
You know some wounds are worse,
    much worse.
           What of the ones

that never heal?
                                You've seen
the wounded waiting for the end
with oxen eyes.
                    Their days
turned infinite as midnights,
and their nights were days;
old actresses whose breasts
as girls were troves—grandfathers
in wheeled chairs who bore
themselves in war like hawks,
their necks defiant and their eyes
snarling.
                Without a word
you thank the God of sickness
for this pause.
                    Returning
to yourself because you must, you
learn you're all you have.
                            You know
your aunt and father faced
a harder darkness with an easier
defiance.
                They let the worst
come on because they knew
it would, regardless.
Thinking of them, you join
    your body in its lair and wait
    for yesterday to turn into the day
    you used to call tomorrow.

Crossing Words Over Crosswords

You're not impelled to name
    the longest rivers in Russia
    even if you know them,
    and you don't.
                      . . . the sixth wife
of Henry the Eighth, the major
port in Sicily, the Spanish
word for blood—all these
strike you as facts best left
to indices.
                  You can live
without them.
                  But the puzzlers
can't, and so you don't.
Dissatisfied with mere completion,
    they resemble seekers who are
    never home because they're always
    going there.
                  Or they're Don Juans
for whom the perfect woman's
not yet met.
                  . . . first letter
of the Hebrew alphabet, an old
Greek coin, Theodore Roosevelt's
middle name, the second highest
peak in Africa. . .
                  Each question's
a mosquito sting you can't ignore.
It does no good to quote
    Diogenes: "Knowledge is not
    intelligence."
                  It does less good
to say you don't know answers
when you do.

The questions linger
in the air like smoke that only
answers will dissolve.
It's just
that mere pursuit, however trivial,
is not your name for leisure.
Raw data doesn't interest you,
and facts in up-and-down
designs don't interest you,
and anything that takes you
north, south, east or west
of now is nowhere near what
interests you.
Better the urge
to taste the world with sight
or hear it into silence
or devour it with both your hands
until the very salt and sniff
of it are yours.
                    . . . inventor
of the cotton gin, the smallest
country in Europe, the six
continents. . .
Just as "a face
is never known until it's loved,"
you know that things will hide
behind your names for them
until you drink them into who
you are.
Your name for danger
is the sureness of the disembodied mind.
As for yourself, you never
learned a lasting thing
until you savored it, and even
then you had your doubts.

No Fanfares, No Handshakes, No Salutes

If "life's a dream with doubts
   about itself," the dreaming
   never stops.
               Regretting
   what you did or did not do
   or always wished to do adds up
   to who you are. . .
             Piaf pretended
   she regretted nothing.
                 One
   genius in his epitaph regretted
   only he was not "the man
   in whose embrace Mathilde Urbach
   swooned."
          An emperor with no
   regrets in middle age
   regretted having no regrets.
Translated, these examples say
   no life is long enough
   nor cosmopolitan enough nor anything
   enough.
         If you desire to see
   your son's daughter's son's
   daughter, you want no less
   than anybody wants.
              Or if you thirst
   to visit everywhere in every
   hemisphere, you mimic old Batuta's
   passion for the next horizon.
Or if you hunger for the maximum,
   you're Faust with all of Faust's
   excesses to remember. . .
             So much
   for dreams.

If you want something
to regret, why not regret you never
once opposed some fluent undermen
we manage to elect—the ideology
or sociology or therapy that people
eat as poetry—the arguments
about theology whose final argument
is *who's the boss*—the righteous
tribes for whom the Renaissance might
just as well have never happened.
Why did you never say that one
good student's worth a thousand
senators?
                    Or that one carpenter
outskills the slitherings of advertisers,
diplomats and other oilers of the word?
Between what you remember
or presume, you're in translation
by whatever keeps translating April
into May, decisions into consequences,
fathers into sons, and you
into whatever.
                    I know
the circumstance.
                    I'm you,
and both of us keep planning
for tomorrow while we're turning
into yesterday.
                    What else
can we conclude except we grow
and die in place despite
our dreams?
                    What is our bounty
but the permanent impermanence
of breath, a shared invisibility,
a gift?

What is our peace
but stopping as we go and talking
for a while of that, just
that, translation to translation?

Understudy

In a world of shadows, you're
   a shadow.
            Each shadow has
a name, and who it's called
is what it does: mechanic,
postman, dentist, President
of these United States, attorney,
acrobat.
            Some mornings
you become your shadow and forget
the self you are.
            Shadowing
shadows or by shadows shadowed,
you pretend all shadows mean
no more than what they mean
to you.
            What's hidden is the animal
within that laughs and bleeds,
luxuriates in kisses, mistakes
what satisfies for what completes
and wonders how its death
will come and where and when.
You've played at shadows long enough
to know a man can die
of order.
            Under every uniforming
face, the life that Aristotle
understood and Shakespeare dramatized
and everybody dies of when it's time
just waits and waits to happen
as it must.
            The fate of islanders
occurs to you.
            For years their seas

seem sisterly.
                          It takes one hurricane
alone to make them ask
which sea is real—the smooth
Sargasso or the waves of nightmare.
The same for Texans.
                          After one
tornado they believe they live
thereafter by the grace of chance
or some indulgence of the wind.
But why go on?
                    Shadow
inside of shadow, the world's
a Chinese box you're always
opening and opening.
                          It proves
the poem of your life will happen
like a poem on a page.
                          It starts
when something else takes over.
Suddenly you're stopped.
                          It's noon,
and not a shadow inks the earth.
You come alive to everything:
the way your fingers shake
a hammer handle like a hand,
the lure of her both breasts
uplifted underwater, children
singing in Spanish, the fluent
silence of the mute.
                          You're both
within and yet above yourself,
and even so the time being
is turning into shadow.
                          Always
Utopian, you keep expecting

more and finding less.
                          You crave
the last impossibilities that lovers
crave—a world devoid
of anything o'clock, freshness
in perpetuity, a holiday from history.
Your shadow waits for you,
      regardless.
                          It's like a suit
you can't outwear and never
will discard.
                          It wants
to wear you now and afterward
and in your grave.
                          You let it wait.

Mediterraneans

Instead of lotus, you can eat
    croissants, brioche, baguettes
    and all the pastries of the sun.
The beach is breasts.
                     Pharmacies
    sell nipplecream in toothpaste
    tubes.
              Beyond Tahiti Beach
    and Pampalone what's visible
    below the navel and above declares
    the final nudities are metaphysical,
    not physical.
                 "*Voulez-vous un parasol!*"
A palace named for Alexandra
    blocks the view Picasso
    savored of the sea in Cannes.
Lebanese outnumber Saudis
    ten to one, and Arabic's
    the second language on the Rue
    d'Antibes.
           "*Unna min Djoun.*
Killna kown min Djoun.
                Lady
    Stanhope lived in Djoun."
A Greek chorus of parked
    yachts is rung with wakes
    from skimmers, cleavers, surfers.
Shucking their tanning mats,
    the swimmers wade, kick,
    crawl, propel themselves
    like frogs or float log-flat
    in tandem.
              The sun paints
    everyone a tawny copper.

"Marvin and me are doing
      Rome tomorrow.
                              One day
      for Rome, then half a day
      for Florence—that's enough."
The nudes that Gauguin painted
      in the real Tahiti made him wonder:
      "Where do we come from, what
      are we, where are we going?"
Here the tourists' answer is,
      "We come from where we come from,
      we're who our passports say
      we are, we're going home."
Under the stars the mistral scatters
      cellophane and kleenex on the sand.
The always-virgin waves seem strewn
      with coins or snow from the moon.
The sea is no one's country.

Who Promised You Tomorrow?

It's time you paganized yourself
    and left all sublimations
    to the dry of soul.
                    It's time
    you learned that ears can taste,
    and eyes remember, and the tongue
    and nostrils see like fingertips
    in any dark.
                    Think back
    or look around, and all you know
    is what your body taught you:
    lake smoke in the Adirondacks,
    the razor's flame across
    your lathered cheek, language
    that changed to silence or to tears
    when there was nothing more
    to say. . .
                    Right here in Cannes
    on the Fourth of July, you watch
    a cornucopia a-swelter in the sun.
A Saudi wife, enrobed
    and cowled like a nun, passes
    a Cannaise in her isosceles
    and thong.
                    They stand there
    like opposed philosophies of women,
    history, desire, God
    and everything you think about
    too much. . .
                    The stationed candles
    on the altar of Notre Dame
    de Bon Voyage diminish
    like your future.
                    Anchored

in the bay, the *S. S. Ticonderoga*
claims the future's now.
Housing a zillion dollars'
    worth of software in her hull,
    she's programed for the war
    that no one wants.
                        She bristles
    like a ploughshare honed into a sword—
    the ultra-weapon from the ultra-tool.
Basking in the hull of your skin
    that shields the software of yourself
    against the worst, you contemplate
    the carefully united states
    you call your body.
                        Concealed
    or bared, it houses who you are,
    and who you are is why you live,
    and why you live is worth
    the life it takes to wonder how.
Your body's not concerned.
                        It answers
    what it needs with breath, sleep,
    love, sweat, roses,
    children and a minimum of thought.
It says all wars are waged
    by puritans, and that the war
    nobody wants is history's excuse
    for every war that ever happened. . .
The gray *Ticonderoga* fires
    a salute of twenty guns
    plus one for independence
    and the men who died to earn it.
Each shot reminds you of the killed
    Americans still left in France.
Before they left their bodies,
    did they think of war or what

their bodies loved and missed
the most: a swim at noon,
the night they kissed a woman
on her mouth, the dawns they waited
for the wind to rise like music,
or the simple freedom of a walk,
a waltz, a trip.
                          Under
the sun of Cannes, you hum
your mind to sleep.
                                    You tell
yourself that time is one
day long or one long day
with pauses for the moon and stars,
and that tomorrow's sun is yesterday's
today.
              Your body answers
that it knows, it's known
for years, it's always known.

French Time

"The French are like that. . ."

A remark *en passant*

Her equally tanned and equal
    breasts repeat the tawny russet
    of the tiles above her balcony.
Her white panties echo
    the whiteness of dreams.

                No dream,
    she waters window-troughs
    of peonies, blow-dries her blonde
    hair and never draws the blinds.
You're watching Wimbledon and her.
Wimbledon's losing.

            A Czech
    spartan and an unacclaimed Australian
    serve, volley and slam
    for Lady Di and half the watching
    world.

        You watch *La Belle Evoque*
    behind her peonies.

              She offers
    what a woman's body offers:
    curvatures, a special poise
    in standing still, legs
    like a dancer's, hair with its own
    loose will, a shoulderblade
    as rudimentary as a wing,
    the inner secrecies.

            At Wimbledon,
    Australia's rallying.

            When you
    look back, *La Belle Evoque's*
    abed.

Beside her lies a man
with arms and shoulders of a stevedore.
A television signal flickers
like a prairie fire across
their touching tans.
                        Australia's
just a point away from triumph.
Suddenly in mid-lob the channel
changes to commercials, news,
and then John Wayne on horseback
saying, "*Bonjour.*"
                        You focus
on the prone-to-proneness game
across the way.
                        Starting at love,
it's now advanced to deuce
or, borrowing from French, *égalité.*
Out suddenly goes the prairie
fire.
            Whatever's happening
in darkness or on British grass
dissolves behind the double fault
of being unexplained and out
of bounds.
                        But this, you tell
yourself, is France.
                        No
explanation is an explanation.
Point.
            Set.
                        Match.

Leafscape

Not "mists and mellow fruitfulness"
    but mulch, drained swimming
    pools, no cookouts
    and the slow glide down
    of nationalities of leaves.
                         It
changes you.
                    It burns away
    what passes for importance: commentators
    playing President—backers
    of cheap housing and expensive
    missiles—bishops caucusing
    like generals who think like corporals.
Persephone's going, and with her
    go tomatoes, robins, rhododendrons,
    baseball and the months of color.
Talking of times to plant
    and reap or times to live and die
    seems now as pointless as philosophy.
Surely Ecclesiastes must have realized
    that all things end, some
    temporarily, and some forever.
Surely you're not the only man
    September sombers while you study
    branches solo-ing in all the scales
    of loss as if the mountains
    were in flames, and you a witness
    mesmerized by fire.
                    No artist
    at his best could mingle pigments
    on a canvas to preserve this blaze
    of music from the drowning snow.
The flames outcolor art.
                Art *is,*

but life *becomes*, and what
it's now becoming is another
life.
 It makes you think
of what it means to go—
go home, go anywhere, go
finally for good.
 With that
to think about, you play the deaf
man listening to leaf-songs
with your eyes.
 You live by listening.

A Man Can Think for Just So Long
Before the Body Wants Its Say

It's not impressed with songs
    that won't stay past, with martyrs
    who will never die, with books
    forever speaking in the present
    tense.
            It lives on breezes
    that become its bones, on kisses
    that abandon it to slaveries
    that set it free, on water
    that reminds it of itself.
                     Give
    it a pear, and it's content.
Deliver it to roses, drumbeats,
    or the fresh truth of bread,
    and it will be your dog.
Why should it wait with you
    for what's to come or what's
    beyond or what's above
    if all its heavens are within?
It craves the immortalities of sense
    that keep a man undying
    while he lives.
                 Its every mouth
    speaks nothing but necessity.
Leave one unsatisfied, and it will
    peak in rages that can start
    a war, abolish populations
    in the name of need, defy
    impossibilities and plunder hemispheres.
Yet always all it seeks is just
    the seesaw-peace of nature's algebra—
    the counterpoint between parfaits
    and pepper, itch and scratch,

phantasmagoria and focus, babble
and song.
                    And what it feels
is yours to savor long before
the Platonist within you says
it's all unreal.
                    The problem is
it's not.
                    The signatures of pain
are legible as print.
                              And Maura's
eyes are unforgettable.
                              And loving
one who loves you back is more
electric than a trillion storms.
And healing, which you quietly
      accept but can't explain,
      is miracle enough to re-create
      the universe…
                    Housed in your body's
universe, you make it
what it makes of you.
                              Pampered,
it softens.
                    Pressured, it toughens.
Summoned, it answers to a name
      as long as answering is possible.
Sickened, it lingers to a close…
Its days are like a book
      left open on a table in the wind.
The wind keeps reading all
      its pages—faster, faster.

Thinking of Afterthinkers

When something happens which they said
would happen, there they are
to say what happened happened
as they said it would.
You say
"the sadness of predestined failure"
isn't absolute, that happiness
is something we can still pursue,
that hope against all hope
is what it means to hope.
No use.
Playing Cassandra suits them
like a smirk. . .
Nor can they be
rebutted since the worst can always
happen when the best is probable
or when the worst is least
expected. . .
Something about them
makes you thirst for air, for ground,
for green.
You ache to smell
the earth's pure salt again
where everything is what it is today,
and every day's today.
Crocuses
that sprout and blossom purple
in an onion snow say blossoming
is worth the gamble.
Somewhere
a spaniel barks and barks
toward a death it never thinks
about. . .
But all these braveries

are blind, predictable.
                    They differ
from the kind that summon us
each day to prove that life
is more than habits done
and done again and added up
like mileage to a grave.
                    Renoir,
near death, kept painting
with a paintbrush taped around
his crippled fingers.
                    Lumumba's
widow, naked to her waistline,
marched behind her husband's bier
and showed the world the brown
defiance of her breasts.
                    Prometheus
stole fire and was praised and damned,
foretelling by the death he risked
for life the price of all salvation.

III   *A Final Gnarled Grain*

The Time It Takes to See

This poem isn't working out.
I want to say that words
    and wonder stay at odds.
                              Feel
    what you see when you see it,
    and the sight's within you.
                                Speak,
    and it's gone.
                   Is it a mystery
to claim we aren't rehearsed
for mystery?
                  When death or joy
or love surprises us, we end
by grieving, talking out of tune
or looking idiotic.
                      Years
afterward we find the words
for what we had no words for
then, which means the past
is simply what we make (re-make)
of it, which means we're always
in arrears.
                We sort our memories
like players who arrange the cards
they're dealt into a kind of order.
Failing even there, we say
    that only artists save the minute
    as it fades.
                  Compared with all
the bronze perfections of Rodin,
we kiss like amateurs, have stances
that are less than statuesque
and dance with all the dignity
of clowns.

99

But why compare?
Rodin the sculptor knew
　　the luxury of second sight
　　and carved with all the flawlessness
　　that retrospect allowed.
　　　　　　　　　　Rodin
　　the man was like the rest of us,
　　knowing the heart can never
　　be prepared for what awaits it,
　　knowing we do the best we can
　　without the option of revision.
Is art mere taxidermy then,
　　a way of re-inventing yesterday
　　into the day we wanted it to be?
Or does the time of seeing
　　happen when we revolutionize past
　　wonder into something we can say?
One way or the other, seeing's
　　not believing any more than
　　listening means only hearing.
Somehow the time at hand
　　must come again when we're
　　composed enough to understand.
If what we've lost by then
　　to living we've regained in gratitude,
　　we've lost as ably as we can.

A Crossing

Boarding this ship of Paul
    the mariner, we bring and find
    our bearings here.
                West
    of our birth and east of death,
    we sail from southern porches
    to the true north of God. . .
Though churches built as ships
    or crosses rise no more,
    we still can tell within these
    walls the time of all cathedrals.
Their bells and trumpets summon
    us to be what we can be
    for the believing.
              Their altars
    prophesy that men who build
    what will outlive them build
    like that first sailor of the Lord
    who christened for the Christ
    he never saw the whole world
    west of Byblos. . .
              If where
    we live the best is when
    we love the most, we sail
    like Paul as far as we can love.
That love's the same in Antioch
    or Chartres or in this sheer
    and steepled prayer.
             The compass
    of this cross shall lead us there.

In a Time of No Answers

If we're like rivers only love
   or suffering can stop for just
   so long, we deepen where we stop
   the longest.
               Afterward we're less
   self-consciously but more ourselves.
We consecrate our words.
                   We walk
   like acolytes.
              We see in all
   we see a prophecy of disappearance.
A nightgown flung like a spent
   lung across a bed sings mutely
   of absence.
             The slow dying
   of old snow remembers how
   we watched it burn from blizzards
   into thaw.
             Careers, distinctions,
   birthdays and the rest dissolve
   like smoke-words scrawled
   by Piper Cubs across the sky.
Outwardly, we're what we were.
Because today's denial is tomorrow's
   truth, we still distrust all versions
   dubbed official.
             We see
   the owl of Minerva fly
   at dusk, which means philosophers
   philosophize when epochs end,
   not helpfully before.
             We watch
   as priests become the butlers of God
   while poets remain God's prodigal

sons, forgivable at last
despite excesses in the name
of love.
                Regardless, the world
of no retreat and no alternative
still stabs us with itself.
Each time we rise from loving,
    satisfied but never quite content,
    we feel the wound.
                        Speaking,
    spoken to or spoken of, we live
    like actors at odd jobs
    between plays.
                    We wonder if the jobs
    or plays are real.
                        As actors we admit
    that skill is greater than strength,
    and art is greater than skill,
    and life is greater than art.
But after that we stop.
Even as the river in us
    tugs us on, we want
    to see the unforeseeable.
We search and search until
    we learn that living best
    means doing what we must with no
    foreknowledge of the outcome.
                                Where
    we are and whom we love
    and how we've come this far
    is all we know.
                    The time
    at hand is immortality enough.
It calls us like a road
    that leads to everything, and so
    we listen, and we go.

103

We Are in All Ways One

Whatever we are, we are
in concentration.
Unable to be
factored further down, we age
like driftwood, sanded thin
by sea and wind into a final
gnarled grain.
But so does
everything.
When God proclaimed,
"I Am Who Am," He said
as much.
In all we do
because we must or all
we just can't do because
we won't, we say the same.
The Jesuit who would not spit
on Christ could not be tortured
into it.
Even after squaws
spooled out his small intestines
while he watched, then fed them
to the dogs, he could not spit.
Tortured or not, we grow
into ourselves so unavoidably
that only death can stop us.
Then history takes over, and the dead
are born again within the loud
applause of tears or in the words
we mint to re-invent their lives.
Meanwhile, the usual evasions. . .
Someone en route will change
his name, his nose, his sex
until the salt of self's

not there at all.
                    We recognize
the signs.
                    The land of contradiction's
all around us.
                    Old people
in young neighborhoods. . .
                              Young
people in old neighborhoods. . .
Fake bacon. . .
                Fake grass. . .
                              Fake talk. . .
What lies beneath the lies
    keeps stirring to be born.
We sit there like an audience
    of one before the world's short
    film gone uncontrollably wild.
Sped up, it's funny.
                    Slowed down,
    it's not.
                Halted in motion,
    it makes us wonder if
    there's more to come, and when. . .
It leaves us wondering until
    we die.
                We can't say why.

Swim Nude, Swim Best

Sporting a nose like a windsock
　　has certain disadvantages.
　　　　　　　　　　　　Kissing's
　　a problem.
　　　　　　　　　Kidding's a nuisance.
Courage concedes Old Warbones
　　loved Roxanne but kept it
　　to himself.
　　　　　　　　　Love says he lacked
　　the courage to proclaim it to her face.
And so the story. . .
　　　　　　　　　　　Stressing
　　the best and hiding the worst
　　did not begin with Bergerac.
Someone is always there
　　to hint we might be ridiculed
　　because we limp or speak
　　with an accent or think we risk
　　repudiation if we write or call
　　or just pretend to care.
　　　　　　　　　　　　Until
　　we act as if it's not, the nose
　　is everybody's curse. . .
　　　　　　　　　　　One day
　　we dive into our lives without
　　a thing to hide like swimmers
　　swimming naked in the dark.
With every stroke we re-invent
　　ourselves.
　　　　　　　　　We populate an element
　　we knew before we knew our names.
The sea becomes a shore,
　　the shore a house, the house
　　a room, the room a bed

where we are more at home
than anywhere.
                        Someone we've loved
forever waits to save us there
while curtains breathe against
themselves like tides, and seawinds
thieve across a windowsill.
We swim from memory to mystery
    and back.
                        It's more than baring
chests and breasts and crotches.
When swimmers love, they shed
    their fear like shame as calmly
    as they take off everything they're
    wearing, even their watches.

Emeritus

"How could I ever sell
      my books," you asked and added,
      "what would I do without them?"
If you were speaking of your very
      sons, you would have said
      the same.
                        Your only sons
were generations of the sons
of others lent to you as students
and retained as friends.
                              Langland,
Chaffee and McPhee...
                              The list
was thirty schoolyears long,
with every year a legacy,
and every legacy as unrepeatable
as birth.
                  Entrusted with so many
      lives that went on living in
and through you after they were gone,
you kept in touch.
                        They wrote.
You spent two hours every day
      to answer them.
                        You quoted
to a few the boast of Sabbatini,
"He was born with the gift
of laughter and a sense that the world
was mad."
                  You loved those mavericks
most who loved and wrestled
with the word.
                  Silent for years,
they'd suddenly appear

as poetry or books you almost
felt you had a hand in writing.
You kept the evidence inscribed
and dated on your shelves.
                                    The Irish
in you filled the rest with all
the best from first-edition Joyce
to Seamus Heaney.
                            Yours
for the consulting or bequeathing, they
waited in their spines like secrets
you would some day share. . .
                                    In a world
where chance is king, a chosen
life like yours becomes as possible
as kindness or fidelity itself—
the one perfection we can earn.
Abundantly at home with books
and first-name friends,
you live alone among the horse-rich
farms and pastures of the few,
wealthier than all that gentry.

                    For Robert W. McGlynn

After Mercutio

Come we to this commemoration
   nude or garbed, we stay
   in most ways one.
                  Midnight
   enshrouds us, and the moon berobes us
   gray and silver to the galaxies.
Black lawns await the sun
   to paint them green again.
The sick are for a time sleep-spared
   the cruelty of roses.
                Swimming
   a sweeter dark, a lover
   lets his fingertips be eyes
   until the lolling one he teases
   sheaths and thighs him to herself.
The kiss of bellies is their
   everything.
             Elsewhere in the easy
   cladding of her skin, a showered
   wife looks west.
               Whatever
   she's observing is composing her.
Cats are afoot.
           Their arch
   stares sparkle sapphire
   in the shadows.
            Listen.
                Volcanoes
   in the sea are spewing ash.
We overhear them as the deaf
   hear detonations with their eyes.
Chocked attics whisper
   to themselves like thieves in corridors.
Isled in the sunlight of the seafall

moon, we beachcomb where we choose
while everything around us
turns into itself.
                    Because
a willow wavers, we believe
in wind, believe in stars
ensorcelled by the same wind,
believe ourselves believing.
We praise the perfect poem
    of a hen's each egg.
                         Platters
    of wet grapes in loose
    erotic sprawls seem irresistible
    as kisses.
                    Rivers arouse
    and reach within us oceans
    far beyond our fathoming.
When we're mad enough
    by all this sorcery, we dance
    fandangos on the shore before
    we sleep.
                    Or else we sing
    the hymm that David sang to Saul
    until the old king woke
    and walked.
                    The world deserves
    that little. . .
                    Nightwords
    like these are not for those
    who love the lies of triumph
    that prevail as history.
                         They're
    for the fools who pry from mystery
    some memory of who we are
    and why we're here.
                         They're for

the mildly bemused and wildly
free.
      For you.
            For me.

To All My Mariners in One

Forget the many who talk
    much, say little, mean
    less and matter least.
                Forget
    we live in times when broadcasts
    of Tchaikovsky's Fifth precede
    announcements of the death
    of tyrants.
            Forget that life
    for governments is priced
    war-cheap but kidnap-high.
Our seamanship is not with such.
From port to port we learn
    that "depths last longer
    than heights," that years are
    meant to disappear like wakes,
    that nothing but the sun stands
    still.
         We share the sweeter
    alphabets of laughter and the slower
    languages of pain.
             Common
    as coal, we find in one another's
    eyes the quiet diamonds
    that are worth the world.
               Drawn
    by the song of our keel, who
    are we but horizons coming true?
Let others wear their memories
    like jewelry.
           We're of the few
    who work apart so well
    together when we must.
             We speak

cathedrals when we speak
and trust no promise but
the pure supremacy of tears.

                                   What
more can we expect?

                                 The sea's
blue mischief may be waiting
for its time and place, but still
we have the stars to guide us.
We have the wind for company.
We have ourselves.

                                 We have
a sailor's faith that says
not even dying can divide us.

Another Word for Time

We speak as people in motion
　　speak, more sure of what's
　　behind us than ahead,
　　but going anyway.
　　　　　　　Trying to see
　　beyond the world we see,
　　we see that seeing's dangerous.
Our props collapse.
　　　　　　　Religion,
　　customs, law, the dream
　　called government. . .
　　　　　　　Nothing
　　sustains us but our eyes and what
　　our eyes, by saying nothing,
　　say.
　　　　　　No wonder Timerman
　　could claim for all of us,
　　"I am at home in subjects
　　now, not countries."
　　　　　　　Before
　　the real frontiers, our passports
　　are invalid.
　　　　　　　They tell us
　　how we're called but never
　　who we are, and who we are's
　　the mystery.
　　　　　　　The pilgrim in us
　　has no fixed address.
　　　　　　　He roams.
He takes us with him when
　　he goes.
　　　　　　Encowled within
　　a fuselage, we speed toward
　　a short tomorrow in another

world.
        We land, speak languages
we almost understand, and trust
in strangers as the best of friends,
and for a time they are.
                        Years
afterward we feel a bond
with them so indestructible
that we're amazed.
                If they
should die, we'd grieve for them
like those old Cuban fishermen
who grieved for Hemingway because
he fished the gulf they fished
and called them friends.
                        With nothing
else to offer him, they gave
the bronze propellors of their
very boats for melting to create
his statue in the plaza of Cojímar. . .
For us the best memorials
are what we heard or read
en route.
                "He's old, but still
in life."
                "Nothing but heart
attack kill Christophine, but why
in the box she so swell up?"
"Cruelty's a mystery and a waste
of pain."
                "I like a dog
that makes you think when you
look at him."
                        "*El Cordobés es
un hombre muy valiente.*"
                        Each word's

a time.
                    Each time's a place.
Each place is where a time
    repeats itself because a word
    returns us there.
                    Crisscrossing
    through the universe the way
    that lightning diagrams the sky,
    we're all companions of the road
    at different altitudes.
                    Here
    in my speeding house below
    the speeding stars, I'm turning
    into language from a pen while you're
    confiding in some traveler you'll
    never see again.
                    The quiet
    bronze of words remembers us.
                            It says
    we were, we are, we will be.